A Little's Book of Carols

Arranged & Illustrated by Rebecca Benjamin

For my babies... I love you with my whole heart.

Love, Mama

Angels We have Heard on High.......page 7

Away in a Manger.......page 11

The First Noel.......page 13

Go, Tell It on the Mountain.......page 27

God Rest Ye Merry, Gentlemen.......page 33

Hark! The Herald Angels Sing.......page 41

Joy to the World.......page 47

O Come, All Ye Faithful.......page 53

O Holy Night.......page 61

O Little Town of Bethlehem.......page 69

Silent Night.......page 75

Twinkle Twinkle Christmas Star.......page 81

We Three Kings.......page 85

While Shepherds Watched Their Flocks.......page 91

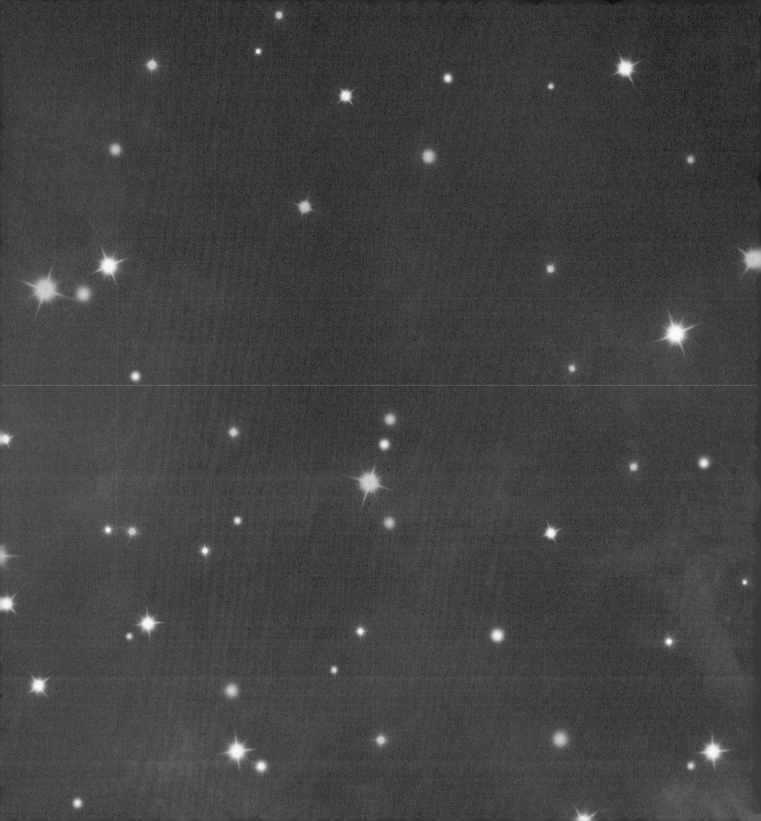

Angels We Have Heard on High

Angels we have heard on high
Sweetly singing o'er the plains,
And the mountains in reply
Echoing their joyous strains.

Gloria, in excelsis Deo!
Gloria, in excelsis Deo!

Shepherds, why this jubilee?
Why your joyous strains prolong?
What the gladsome tidings be
Which inspire your heavenly song?

Gloria, in excelsis Deo!
Gloria, in excelsis Deo!

Come to Bethlehem and see
Christ whose birth the angels sing;
Come, adore on bended knee,
Christ the Lord, the newborn King.

Gloria, in excelsis Deo!
Gloria, in excelsis Deo!

See Him in a manger laid,
Whom the choirs of angels praise;
Mary, Joseph, lend your aid,
While our hearts in love we raise.

Gloria, in excelsis Deo!
Gloria, in excelsis Deo!

Angels We Have Heard on High

1. An - gels we have heard on high Sweet - ly sing - ing o'er the plains,
2. Shep - herds, why this ju - bi - lee? Why your joy - ous strains pro - long?
3. Come to Beth - le - hem and see Christ Whose birth the an - gels sing;
4. See Him in a man - ger laid, Whom the choirs of an - gels praise;

And the moun - tains in re - ply E - cho - ing their joy - ous strains.
What the glad - some tid - ings be Which in - spire your heaven - ly song? Glor-
Come, a - dore on bend - ed knee, Christ the Lord, the new - born King.
Mar - y, Jo - seph, lend your aid, While our hearts in love we raise.

i - a, in ex - cel - sis De - o! Glor-

i - a, in ex - cel - sis De - o!

11

Away in a Manger

Away in a manger,
No crib for a bed,
The little Lord Jesus
Laid down His sweet head.
The stars in the sky
Looked down where He lay,
The little Lord Jesus,
Asleep on the hay.

The cattle are lowing,
The Baby awakes,
But little Lord Jesus,
No crying He makes;
I love Thee, Lord Jesus,
Look down from the sky
And stay by my cradle
Till morning is nigh.

Be near me, Lord Jesus,
I ask Thee to stay
Close by me forever,
And love me, I pray;
Bless all the dear children
In Thy tender care,
And fit us for Heaven
To live with Thee there.

Away in a Manger

♩=115

1. A - way in a man-ger, no crib for a bed, The lit - tle Lord Je - sus laid
2. The cat - tle are low-ing, the Ba - by a - wakes, But lit - tle Lord Je - sus, no
3. Be near me, Lord Je - sus, I ask Thee to stay Close by me for - ev - er, and

down His sweet head. The stars in the sk - y looked down where He lay, The
cry - ing He makes; I love Thee, Lord Je - sus, look down from the sky And
love me, I pray; Bless all the dear child-ren in Thy ten - der care, And

lit - tle Lord Je - sus, a - sleep on the hay.
stay by my cra - dle til morn-ing is nigh.
fit us for heav-en to live with Thee there.

The First Noel

The first Noel the angel did say
Was to certain poor shepherds
In fields as they lay;
In fields where they lay tending their sheep,
On a cold winter's night that was so deep.

Noel, Noel, Noel, Noel,
Born is the King of Israel.

They looked up and saw a star
Shining in the east,
Beyond them far;
And to the earth it gave great light,
And so it continued both day and night.

Noel, Noel, Noel, Noel,
Born is the King of Israel.

And by the light of that same star
Three wise men came
From country far;
To seek for a king was their intent,
And to follow the star wherever it went.

Noel, Noel, Noel, Noel,
Born is the King of Israel.

This star drew nigh to the northwest,
Over Bethlehem
It took its rest;
And there it did both stop and stay,
Right over the place where Jesus lay.

Noel, Noel, Noel, Noel,
Born is the King of Israel.

Then did they know assuredly
Within that house
The King did lie;
One entered it them for to see,
And found the Babe in poverty.

Noel, Noel, Noel, Noel,
Born is the King of Israel.

Then entered in those wise men three,
Full reverently
Upon the knee,
And offered there, in His presence,
Their gold and myrrh and frankincense.

Noel, Noel, Noel, Noel,
Born is the King of Israel.

Between an ox stall and an ass,
This Child truly
There He was;
For want of clothing they did Him lay
All in a manger, among the hay.

Noel, Noel, Noel, Noel,
Born is the King of Israel.

Then let us all with one accord
Sing praises to
Our heavenly Lord;
That hath made Heaven and earth of naught,
And with His blood mankind hath bought.

Noel, Noel, Noel, Noel,
Born is the King of Israel

If we in our time shall do well,
We shall be free
From death and hell;
For God hath prepared for us all
A resting place in general.

Noel, Noel, Noel, Noel,
Born is the King of Israel.

The First Noel

1. The first No - el the an - gel did say Was to cer - tain poor shep - herds in
2. They look - èd up and sa - w a star Shin - ing i - n the ea - st, be-
3. And by the light of th - at same star Three wi - se men ca - me from co-
4. This star drew nigh to th - e north - west, O' - er Be - th - le - he - m it
5. Then en - tered in those wi - se men three, Ful - l re - v - er - ent - ly up-

fields as they lay. In fields where they lay keep - ing their sheep, On a cold win - ter's
- yo - nd them far; And to the earth it ga - ve great light, A - nd so it con-
- un - try far; To seek for a king was the - ir in - tent, And to fol - low the
- o - ok its rest; And there it did both st - op a - nd stay, Right o - ver the
- o - n the knee; And of - fered there, in H - is pre - sence, Their go - ld and my-

Refrain

ni - ght that was so deep.
- tin - ued both day and night.
star wher - ev - er it went. No - el, No - el, No - el, No - el, Born is the King of
pl - ace where Je - sus lay.
- rhh and fr - ank - in - cense.

Is - ra - el.

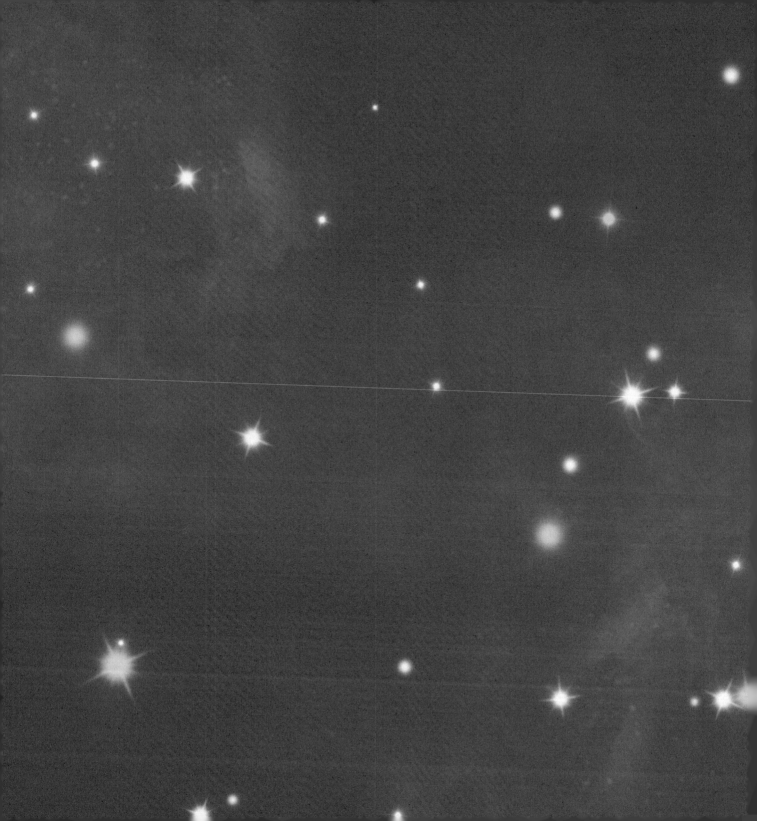

Go, Tell It on the Mountain

Go, tell it on the mountain,
Over the hills and everywhere
Go, tell it on the mountain,
That Jesus Christ is born.

While shepherds kept their watching
O'er silent flocks by night
Behold throughout the heavens
There shone a holy light.

Go, tell it on the mountain,
Over the hills and everywhere
Go, tell it on the mountain,
That Jesus Christ is born.

The shepherds feared and trembled,
When lo! above the earth,
Rang out the angel chorus
That hailed the Savior's birth.

Go, tell it on the mountain,
Over the hills and everywhere
Go, tell it on the mountain,
That Jesus Christ is born.

Down in a lowly manger
The humble Christ was born
And God sent us salvation
That blessed Christmas morn.

Go, tell it on the mountain,
Over the hills and everywhere
Go, tell it on the mountain,
That Jesus Christ is born.

Go, Tell It on the Mountain

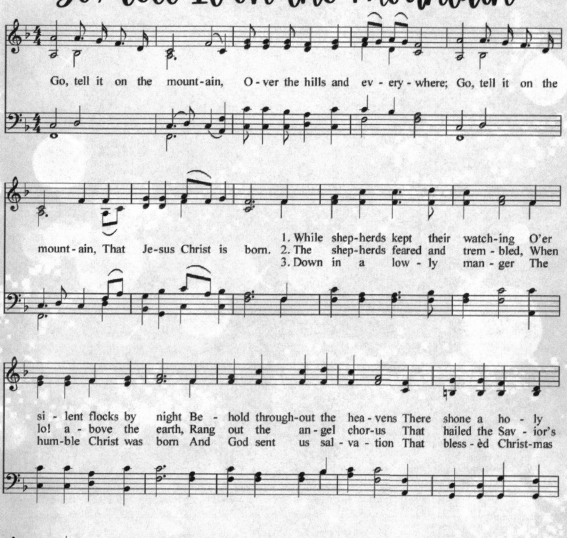

Go, tell it on the mount-ain, O-ver the hills and ev-ery-where; Go, tell it on the mount-ain, That Je-sus Christ is born.

1. While shep-herds kept their watch-ing O'er
2. The shep-herds feared and trem-bled, When
3. Down in a low-ly man-ger The

si-lent flocks by night Be-hold through-out the hea-vens There shone a ho-ly
lo! a-bove the earth, Rang out the an-gel chor-us That hailed the Sav-ior's
hum-ble Christ was born And God sent us sal-va-tion That bless-èd Christ-mas

light.
birth.
morn.

God Rest ye
Merry, Gentlemen

God rest ye merry, gentlemen,
Let nothing you dismay,
Remember Christ our Savior
Was born on Christmas Day;
To save us all from Satan's power
When we were gone astray.

O tidings of comfort and joy,
Comfort and joy;
O tidings of comfort and joy.

In Bethlehem, in Israel,
This blessed Babe was born,
And laid within a manger
Upon this blessed morn;
The which His mother Mary
Did nothing take in scorn.

O tidings of comfort and joy,
Comfort and joy;
O tidings of comfort and joy.

From God our heavenly Father
A blessed angel came;
And unto certain shepherds
Brought tidings of the same;
How that in Bethlehem was born
The Son of God by name.

O tidings of comfort and joy,
Comfort and joy;
O tidings of comfort and joy.

Fear not, then, said the angel,
Let nothing you affright
This day is born a Savior
Of a pure Virgin bright,
To free all those who trust in Him
From Satan's power and might.

O tidings of comfort and joy,
Comfort and joy;
O tidings of comfort and joy.

The shepherds at those tidings
Rejoiced much in mind,
And left their flocks a-feeding
In tempest, storm and wind,
And went to Bethl'em straightaway
This blessed Babe to find.

O tidings of comfort and joy,
Comfort and joy;
O tidings of comfort and joy.

But when to Bethlehem they came
Where our dear Savior lay,
They found Him in a manger
Where oxen feed on hay;
His mother Mary kneeling
Unto the Lord did pray.

O tidings of comfort and joy,
Comfort and joy;
O tidings of comfort and joy.

Now to the Lord sing praises
All you within this place,
And with true love and brotherhood
Each other now embrace;
This holy tide of Christmas
All others doth deface.

O tidings of comfort and joy,
Comfort and joy;
O tidings of comfort and joy.

God bless the ruler of this house,
And send him long to reign,
And many a merry Christmas
May live to see again;
Among your friends and kindred
That live both far and near—

That God send you a happy new year,
Happy new year,
And God send you a happy new year.

God Rest Ye Merry, Gentlemen

1. God rest ye merry, gentlemen, let nothing you dismay, Remember Christ our Savior was born on Christmas Day; To save us all from Satan's power when we were gone astray.
2. In Bethlehem, in Israel, this blessèd Babe was born, And laid within a manger upon this blessèd morn; The which His mother Mary did nothing take in scorn.
3. From God our heavenly Father a blessèd angel came; And unto certain shepherds brought tidings of the same; How that in Bethlehem was born the Son of God by name.
4. "Fear not, then," said the angel, "Let nothing you affright This day is born a Savior of a pure virgin bright, To free all those who trust in Him from Satan's power and might." O tidings of
5. The shepherds at those tidings rejoiced much in mind, And left their flocks a-feeding in tempest, storm and wind, And went to Beth'lem straightaway this blessèd Babe to find.
6. But when to Bethlehem they came where our dear Savior lay, They found Him in a manger where oxen feed on hay; His mother Mary kneeling unto the Lord did pray.
7. Now to the Lord sing praises all you within this place, And with true love and brotherhood each other now embrace; This holy tide of Christmas all others doth deface.
8. God bless the ruler of this house, and send him long to reign, And many a merry Christmas may live to see again; Among your friends and kindred that live both far and near.

Refrain

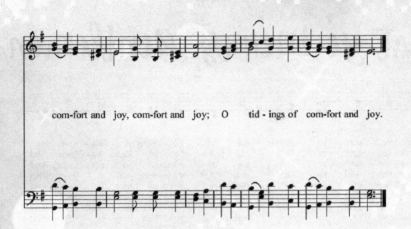

com-fort and joy, com-fort and joy; O tid - ings of com-fort and joy.

Hark! The Herald Angels Sing

Hark! The herald angels sing,
Glory to the newborn King;
Peace on earth, and mercy mild,
God and sinners reconciled!
Joyful, all ye nations rise,
Join the triumph of the skies;
With th'angelic host proclaim,
Christ is born in Bethlehem!

Hark! the herald angels sing,
Glory to the newborn King!

Christ, by highest Heav'n adored;
Christ the everlasting Lord;
Late in time, behold Him come,
Offspring of a virgin's womb.
Veiled in flesh the Godhead see;
Hail th'incarnate Deity,
Pleased with us in flesh to dwell,
Jesus our Emmanuel.

Hark! the herald angels sing,
Glory to the newborn King!

Hail the heav'nly Prince of Peace!
Hail the Sun of Righteousness!
Light and life to all He brings,
Ris'n with healing in His wings.
Mild He lays His glory by,
Born that man no more may die.
Born to raise the sons of earth,
Born to give them second birth.

Hark! the herald angels sing,
Glory to the newborn King!

Come, Desire of nations, come,
Fix in us Thy humble home;
Rise, the woman's conqu'ring Seed,
Bruise in us the serpent's head.
Now display Thy saving power,
Ruined nature now restore;
Now in mystic union join
Thine to ours, and ours to Thine.

Hark! the herald angels sing,
Glory to the newborn King!

Adam's likeness, Lord, efface,
Stamp Thine image in its place:
Second Adam from above,
Reinstate us in Thy love.
Let us Thee, though lost, regain,
Thee, the Life, the inner man:
O, to all Thyself impart,
Formed in each believing heart.

Hark! the herald angels sing,
Glory to the newborn King!

Hark! The Herald Angels Sing

Joy to the World

Joy to the world; the Lord is come;
Let earth receive her king:
Let every heart prepare Him room,
And Heaven and nature sing,
And Heaven and nature sing,
And Heaven, and Heaven, and nature sing.

Joy to the earth, the Savior reigns;
Let men their songs employ;
While fields and floods, rocks, hills and plains
Repeat the sounding joy,
Repeat the sounding joy,
Repeat, repeat, the sounding joy.

No more let sins and sorrows grow,
Nor thorns infest the ground;
He comes to make His blessings flow
Far as the curse is found,
Far as the curse is found,
Far as, far as, the curse is found.

He rules the world with truth and grace,
And makes the nations prove
The glories of His righteousness,
And wonders of His love,
And wonders of His love,
And wonders, wonders, of His love.

Joy to the World

O Come, All ye Faithful

O come, all ye faithful,
Joyful and triumphant,
O come ye, O come ye,
To Bethlehem.
Come and behold Him,
Born the King of angels;

O come, let us adore Him,
O come, let us adore Him,
O come, let us adore Him,
Christ the Lord.

True God of true God
Light from Light Eternal,
Lo, He shuns not
The Virgin's womb;
Son of the Father,
Begotten, not created;

O come, let us adore Him,
O come, let us adore Him,
O come, let us adore Him,
Christ the Lord.

Sing, choirs of angels,
Sing in exultation;
O sing, all ye citizens
Of Heaven above!
Glory to God, all
Glory in the highest;

O come, let us adore Him,
O come, let us adore Him,
O come, let us adore Him,
Christ the Lord.

See how the shepherds,
Summoned to His cradle,
Leaving their flocks,
Draw nigh to gaze;
We too will thither
Bend our joyful footsteps;

O come, let us adore Him,
O come, let us adore Him,
O come, let us adore Him,
Christ the Lord.

Lo! star led chieftains,
Magi, Christ adoring,
Offer Him incense,
Gold, and myrrh;
We to the Christ Child
Bring our hearts' oblations.

O come, let us adore Him,
O come, let us adore Him,
O come, let us adore Him,
Christ the Lord.

Child, for us sinners
Poor and in the manger,
We would embrace Thee,
With love and awe;
Who would not love Thee,
Loving us so dearly?

O come, let us adore Him,
O come, let us adore Him,
O come, let us adore Him,
Christ the Lord.

Yea, Lord, we greet Thee,
Born this happy morning;
Jesus, to Thee be all glory given;
Word of the Father,
Now in flesh appearing.

O come, let us adore Him,
O come, let us adore Him,
O come, let us adore Him,
Christ the Lord.

O Come, All ye Faithful

♩=115

1. O come, all ye faith-ful, joy-ful and tri-um-phant, O come ye, O
2. True God of true God, Light from Light E-ter-nal, Lo, He
3. Sing, choirs of an-gels, sing in ex-ul-ta-tion; O sing, all ye
4. See how the shep-herds, sum-moned to His cra-dle, Leaving their
5. Lo! star led chief-tains, Ma-gi, Christ a-dor-ing, Of-fer Him
6. Child, for us sin-ners poor and in the man-ger, We would em-
7. Yea, Lord, we greet Thee, born this hap-py morn-ing; Je-sus,

come ye, to Beth-le-hem. Come and be-hold Him, born the King of an-gels;
shuns not the Vir-gin's womb; Son of the Fa-ther, be-got-ten, not creat-ed;
citi-zens of Heaven a-bove! Glo-ry to God, all glo-ry in the high-est;
flocks, draw nigh to gaze; We too will thi-ther bend our joy-ful foot-steps;
in-cense, gold, and myrrh; We to the Christ Child bring our hearts' o-bla-tions.
-brace Thee, with love and awe; Who would not love Thee, lov-ing us so dear-ly?
to Thee be all glo-ry giv'n; Word of the Fa-ther, now in flesh ap-pear-ing.

Refrain

O come, let us a-dore Him, O come, let us a-dore Him, O come, let us a-dore Him, Christ

the Lord.

O Holy Night

O holy night, the stars are brightly shining;
It is the night of the dear Savior's birth!
Long lay the world in sin and error pining,
Till He appeared and the soul felt its worth.
A thrill of hope, the weary soul rejoices,
For yonder breaks a new and glorious morn.
Fall on your knees, O hear the angel voices!
O night divine, O night when Christ was born!
O night, O holy night, O night divine!

Led by the light of a faith serenely beaming,
With glowing hearts by His cradle we stand.
So led by light of a star so sweetly gleaming,
Here came the wise men from Orient land.
The King of kings lay thus in lowly manger,
In all our trials born to be our friend!
He knows our need—to our weakness is no stranger.
Behold your king; before Him lowly bend!
Behold your king; before Him lowly bend!

Truly He taught us to love one another;
His law is love and His Gospel is peace.
Chains shall He break, for the slave is our brother
And in His name all oppression shall cease.
Sweet hymns of joy in grateful chorus raise we,
Let all within us praise His holy name!
Christ is the Lord! O praise His name forever!
His pow'r and glory evermore proclaim!
His pow'r and glory evermore proclaim!

O Holy Night

1. O ho - ly night, the stars are bright - ly
2. Led by the light of a faith se - rene - ly
3. Tru - ly He taught us to love one an-

shin - ing; It is the night of the dear Sav - ior's
beam - ing, With glow - ing hearts by His cra - dle we
- o - ther; His law is love and His Gos - pel is

birth! Long lay the
stand. So led by
peace. Chains shall He

world in sin and er-ror pin - ing, Till He ap-
light of a star so sweet-ly gleam - ing, Here came the
break, for the slave is our bro - ther And in His

-peared and the soul felt its worth. A
wise men from Or - i - ent land. The
name all op-pres-sion shall cease. Sweet

thrill of hope, the wea-ry soul re-joic-es, For
King of kings lay thus in low-ly man-ger, In
hymns of joy in grate-ful chor-us raise we, Let

yon - der breaks a new and glor-ious morn.
all our tri - als born to be our friend!
all with - in us praise His ho - ly name!

Fall on your knees, O hear the an-gel
He knows our need— to our weak-ness is no
Christ is the Lord! O praise His name for-

voic-es! O night di-vine, O night when Christ was born! O
stran-ger. Be-hold your king; be-fore Him low-ly bend! Be-
-ev-er! His pow'r and glo-ry ev-er-more pro-claim! His

night, O ho-ly night, O night di-vine!
-hold your king; be-fore Him low-ly bend!
pow'r and glo-ry ev-er-more pro-claim!

night, O
hold your
pow'r and

67

ho - ly night, O night di - vine!
king;   be - fore Him low - ly bend!
glo - ry ev - er - more pro - claim!

O Little Town of Bethlehem

O little town of Bethlehem,
How still we see thee lie!
Above thy deep and dreamless sleep
The silent stars go by.
Yet in thy dark streets shineth
The everlasting Light;
The hopes and fears of all the years
Are met in thee tonight.

For Christ is born of Mary,
And gathered all above,
While mortals sleep, the angels keep
Their watch of wondering love.
O morning stars together,
Proclaim the holy birth,
And praises sing to God the King,
And peace to men on earth!

How silently, how silently,
The wondrous Gift is giv'n;
So God imparts to human hearts
The blessings of His Heav'n.
No ear may hear His coming,
But in this world of sin,
Where meek souls will receive Him still,
The dear Christ enters in.

Where children pure and happy
Pray to the blessed Child,
Where misery cries out to Thee,
Son of the mother mild;
Where charity stands watching
And faith holds wide the door,
The dark night wakes, the glory breaks,
And Christmas comes once more.

O holy Child of Bethlehem,
Descend to us, we pray;
Cast out our sin, and enter in,
Be born in us today.
We hear the Christmas angels
The great glad tidings tell;
O come to us, abide with us,
Our Lord Emmanuel!

O Little Town of Bethlehem

♩=105

1. O lit-tle town of Bethle-hem, how still we see thee lie! A-
2. For Christ is born of Ma-ry, and ga-thered all a-bove, While
3. How si-lent-ly, how silent-ly, the won-drous Gift is giv'n; So
4. Where child-ren pure and hap-py pray to the bless-èd Child, Where
5. O ho-ly Child of Bethle-hem, de-scend to us, we pray; Cast

-bove thy deep and dream-less sleep the si-lent stars go by. Yet
mor-tals sleep, the an-gels keep their watch of won-dering love. O
God im-parts to hu-man hearts the bless-ings of His heav'n. No
mis-er-y cries out to Thee, Son of the mo-ther mild; Where
out our sin, and en-ter in, be born in us to-day. We

in thy dark streets shin-eth the ev-er-last-ing Light; The
morn-ing stars to-ge-ther, pro-claim the ho-ly birth, And
ear may hear His com-ing, but in this world of sin, Where
char-i-ty stands watch-ing and faith holds wide the door, The
hear the Christ-mas an-gels the great glad tid-ings tell; O

hopes and fears of all the years are met in thee to-night.
prais-es sing to God the King, and peace to men on earth!
meek souls will re-ceive Him still, the dear Christ en-ters in.
dark night wakes, the glor-y breaks, and Christ-mas comes once more.
come to us, a-bide with us, our Lord Em-man-u-el!

Silent Night

Silent night, holy night,
All is calm, all is bright
Round yon virgin mother and Child.
Holy Infant, so tender and mild,
Sleep in heavenly peace,
Sleep in heavenly peace.

Silent night, holy night,
Shepherds quake at the sight;
Glories stream from heaven afar,
Heavenly hosts sing Alleluia!
Christ the Savior is born,
Christ the Savior is born!

Silent night, holy night,
Son of God, love's pure light;
Radiant beams from Thy holy face
With the dawn of redeeming grace,
Jesus, Lord, at Thy birth,
Jesus, Lord, at Thy birth.

Silent night, holy night
Wondrous star, lend thy light;
With the angels let us sing,
Alleluia to our king;
Christ the Savior is born,
Christ the Savior is born!

Silent Night

♩=50

1. Si - lent night, ho - ly night, All is calm, all is bright Round yon vir - gin
2. Si - lent night, ho - ly night, Shep - herds quake at the sight; Glo - ries stream from
3. Si - lent night, ho - ly night, Son of God, love's pure Light; Ra - diant beams from
4. Si - lent night, ho - ly night, Wond-rous star, lend thy light; With the an - gels

mo - ther and Child. Ho - ly In - fant, so ten-der and mild, Sleep in hea - ven-ly peace,
heav-en a - far, Heav'n-ly ho - sts sing Al - le - lu - ia! Christ the Sa - vior is born,
Thy ho - ly face With the dawn of re - de - em-ing grace, Je - sus, Lord, at Thy birth,
le - t us sing, Al - le-l - u - ia t - o our king; Christ the Sav - ior is born,

Sleep in heav - en - ly peace.
Christ the Sa - vior is born!
Je - sus, Lord, at Thy birth.
Christ the Sav - ior is born.

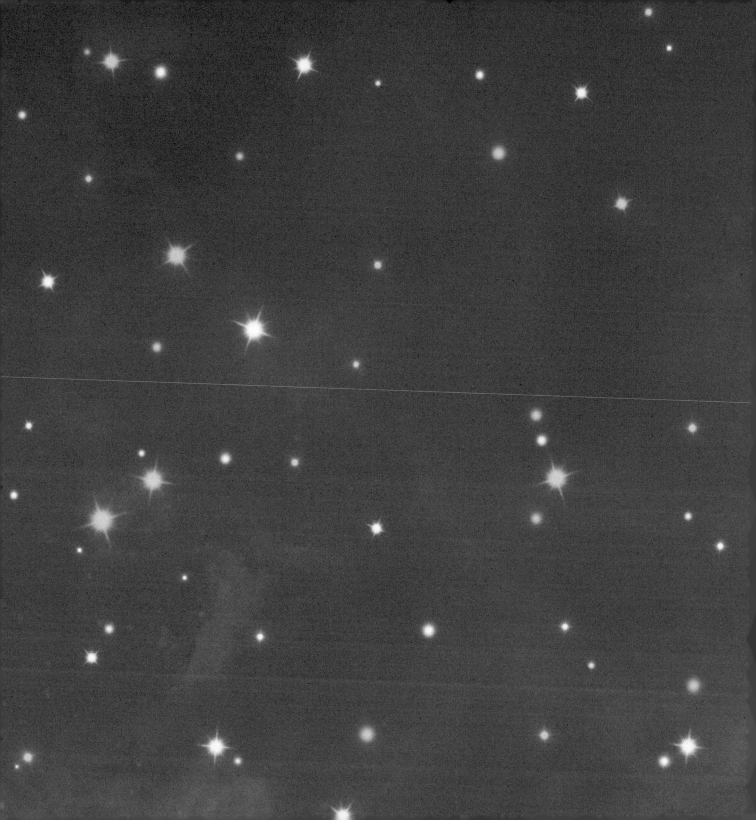

Twinkle, Twinkle, Christmas Star

Twinkle, twinkle, Christmas star!
Who can tell me what you are?
Up above the world so high,
Like a diamond in the sky?

Always show your bright, clear light;
Shine and sparkle thro' the night;
Twinkle, twinkle, little star,
How I wonder what you are.

When the golden day is done,
And the night is just begun,
Then I'll wait and watch for you,
As you twinkle thro' the blue.

Always show your bright, clear light;
Shine and sparkle thro' the night;
Twinkle, twinkle, little star,
How I wonder what you are.

When the night grows dark and chill,
Then you shine more bright and still,
And your kindly watch you keep
While the little children sleep.

Always show your bright, clear light;
Shine and sparkle thro' the night;
Twinkle, twinkle, little star,
How I wonder what you are.

Little star, with you I'd shine,
To His praise who is divine;
Jesus is our glorious king;
For Him children love to sing.

Always show your bright, clear light;
Shine and sparkle thro' the night;
Twinkle, twinkle, little star,
How I wonder what you are.

We Three Kings

We three kings of Orient are;
Bearing gifts we traverse afar,
Field and fountain, moor and mountain,
Following yonder star.

O star of wonder, star of light,
Star with royal beauty bright,
Westward leading, still proceeding,
Guide us to thy perfect light.

Born a king on Bethlehem's plain
Gold I bring to crown Him again,
King forever, ceasing never,
Over us all to reign.

O star of wonder, star of light,
Star with royal beauty bright,
Westward leading, still proceeding,
Guide us to thy perfect light.

Frankincense to offer have I;
Incense owns a deity nigh;
Prayer and praising, voices raising,
Worshipping God on high.

O star of wonder, star of light,
Star with royal beauty bright,
Westward leading, still proceeding,
Guide us to thy perfect light.

Myrrh is mine, its bitter perfume
Breathes a life of gathering gloom;
Sorrowing, sighing, bleeding, dying,
Sealed in the stone cold tomb.

O star of wonder, star of light,
Star with royal beauty bright,
Westward leading, still proceeding,
Guide us to thy perfect light.

Glorious now behold Him arise;
King and God and sacrifice;
Alleluia, Alleluia,
Sounds through the earth and skies.

O star of wonder, star of light,
Star with royal beauty bright,
Westward leading, still proceeding,
Guide us to thy perfect light

We Three Kings

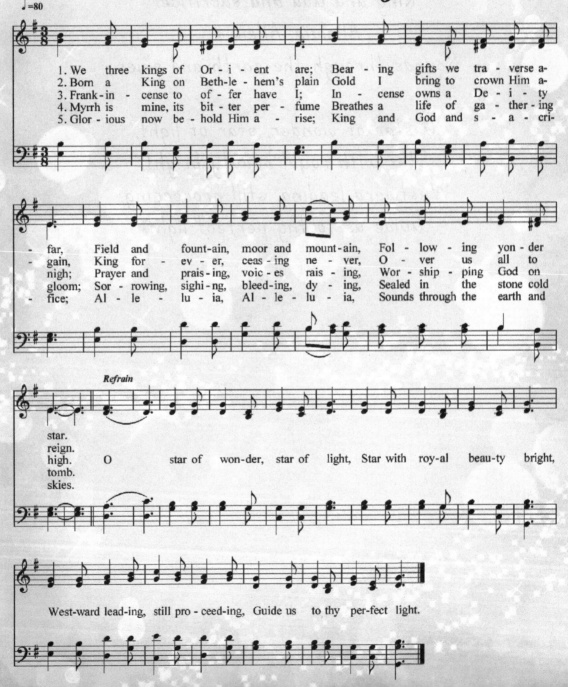

While Shepherds Watched Their Flocks

While shepherds watched their flocks by night,
All seated on the ground,
The angel of the Lord came down,
And glory shone around,
And glory shone around.

Fear not! said he, for mighty dread
Had seized their troubled mind.
"Glad tidings of great joy I bring
To you and all mankind
To you and all mankind.

"To you, in David's town, this day
Is born of David's line
A Savior, who is Christ the Lord,
And this shall be the sign,
And this shall be the sign.

The heavenly Babe you there shall find
To human view displayed,
All meanly wrapped in swathing bands,
And in a manger laid,
And in a manger laid.

Thus spake the seraph and forthwith
Appeared a shining throng
Of angels praising God on high,
Who thus addressed their song,
Who thus addressed their song:

All glory be to God on high,
And to the Earth be peace;
Good will henceforth from Heav'n to men
Begin and never cease,
Begin and never cease!

While Shepherds Watched Their Flocks

♩=108

1. While shep - herds watched their flocks by night, All seat - ed on the ground, The
2. "Fear not!" said he, for might - y dread Had seized their trou - bled mind. "Glad
3. "To you, in Da - vid's town, this day Is born of Da - vid's line A
4. "The heav - en - ly Babe you there shall find To hu - man view dis - played, All
5. Thus spake the ser - aph and forth - with Ap - peared a shin - ing throng Of
6. "All glo - ry be to God on high, And to the Earth be peace; Good

an - gel of the Lord came down, And glo - ry shone a - round, And
tid - ings of great joy I bring To you and all man - kind To
Sav - ior, who is Christ the Lord, And this shall be the sign, And
mean - ly wrapped in swath - ing bands, And in a man - ger laid, And
an - gels prais - ing God on high, Who thus ad - dressed their song, Who
will hence - forth from Heav'n to men Be - gin and ne - ver cease, Be-

glo - ry shone a - round.
you and all man - kind.
this shall be the sign.
in a man - ger laid."
thus ad - dressed their song:
- gin and ne - ver cease!"

Angels We Have Heard on High
Words: Traditional French carol. Translated from French to English by James Chadwick, 1862.
Music: French carol tune, arranged by Edward S. Barnes, 1919

Away in a Manger
Words: Verses 1 & 2, Anonymous, 1885. Verse 3 written by John T. McFarland.
Music: James R. Murray, 1887

The First Noel
Words & Music: Traditional English carol. This combination of music and lyrics first appeared in 1883.

Go, Tell it on the Mountain
Words: John W. Work, Jr., 1907
Music: African-American Spiritual

God Rest Ye Merry, Gentlemen
Words & Music: Traditional English carol

Hark! The Herald Angels Sing
Words: Charles Wesley, 1739
Music: Felix Mendelssohn, 1840

Joy to the World
Words: Isaac Watts, 1719
Music: Arranged by Lowell Mason, 1836

O Come, All Ye Faithful
Words: Verses 1 through 3, John F. Wade, 1743. Verses 1 through 3 were translated from Latin to English by
Frederick Oakley, 1841. Verses 4 & 6 written by Etienne Jean Francois Borderies, 1794. Verses 5 & 7,
Anonymous. Verses 4 through 7 were translated to English by William T. Brooke, 1884.
Music: Anonymous, variously attributed to John Wade, John Reading, or Marco Antonio Simao

O Holy Night
Words: Placide Cappeau, 1843. Translated from French to English by John S. Dwight, 1855.
Music: Adolphe C. Adam, 1843

O Little Town of Bethlehem
Words: Phillips Brooks, 1867
Music: Lewis H. Redner, 1868

Silent Night
Words: Josef Mohr, 1818. Verses 1 & 3 were translated from German to English by John F. Young, 1863.
Anonymous translator for verses 2 & 4.
Music: Franz X. Gruber, 1820

Twinkle, Twinkle, Christmas Star
Words: Grace C. Warren, 1893. The lyrics are adapted from the poem "The Star", written by Jane Taylor,
1806.

We Three Kings
Words & Music: John H. Hopkins, Jr., 1857

While Shepherds Watched Their Flocks
Words: Nahum Tate, 1700
Music: George F. Handel, 1728

14391234R00057